T0199060

AuthorHouse™
1663 Liberty Drive
Bloomington, IN 47403
www.authorhouse.com
Phone: 833-262-8899

Because of the dynamic nature of the Internet, any web addresses or links contained in this book may have changed since publication and may no longer be valid. The views expressed in this work are solely those of the author and do not necessarily reflect the views of the publisher, and the publisher hereby disclaims any responsibility for them.

This book is printed on acid-free paper.

ISBN: 978-1-6655-6964-4 (sc)
ISBN: 978-1-6655-6965-1 (e)

Print information available on the last page.

Published by AuthorHouse   10/27/2022

authorHOUSE®

Over half a million people graduate from hunter education every year in the United States, and through this educational program, both youth and adults learn important lessons focusing on ethics, safe firearm handling, conservation, and a hunter's responsibility as a steward of conservation.

Chris's First Hunting Adventure demonstrates how all these lessons can be applied in the field while capturing the excitement and thrill of spending time in the wilderness with family and friends. When someone decides to become a responsible hunter, they are also making a commitment to strengthen their connection to the natural world by spending more time outdoors and respecting their place within it.

Throughout the book, Chris is faced with difficult decisions, and his preparedness and education allow him to overcome challenges resulting in an unforgettable experience. It's easy to imagine yourself or your friend having a similar adventure. It all starts with hunter education and the decision to enter an exciting activity that offers both challenges and rewards not found in other recreational choices.

All states offer hunter education programs, and your hunter education card becomes your passport to opportunities all over the world through an international community. There are more opportunities than ever before through your state wildlife agency and their partner organizations to hone your skills in the outdoors, find a hunting mentor, and begin your journey just like Chris.

I wish you success with this book and success to all your readers in the field. Be safe, responsible, ethical, and have fun just like Chris and his family. Join the hunt today!

Sincerely,

Alex Baer
Executive Director, IHEA-USA

The Big Day

had arrived when Chris received his Hunter's Education Graduate Card. He was excited to show his mom and dad his achievement. His real adventure and excitement was just about to begin.

HEY DAD! I GOT IT I GOT IT!

Chris, I know how hard you studied to get your Hunter Education Graduate Card... Now your Mom and I have a surprise for you in the house.

ALL RIGHT!

WOW... COOL!!!

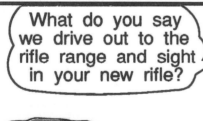

What do you say we drive out to the rifle range and sight in your new rifle?

GREAT!

As they drive along Chris' dad explains the responsibilty and privilege of owning his own rifle and to always respect others and always keep the law.

They set the target in front of the hill at the rifle range...

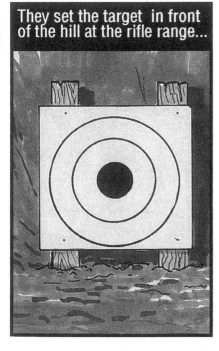

Chris sets himself, takes steady aim...

BULLSEYE!

POW

GOOD GROUP!

WHAM

BANG

GOOD SHOT!

Why would Chris' dad want him to fire his new rifle before he goes out deer hunting?

- They had plenty of ammunition?
- He wanted him to become familiar with his new rifle?
- They just wanted to shoot for fun?

1

WHY IS IT VERY IMPORTANT TO SET THE PRACTICE TARGET IN FRONT OF A HILL OR MOUND?

☐ A dirty rifle can become jammed and dangerous to hunt with.

☐ Cleaning it will make it look good.

☐ It will keep it rust free and in good working order.

2

It's now two days before the start of the deer hunting season, and they have been preparing their hunting and camping gear. Now, just a few things left to do.

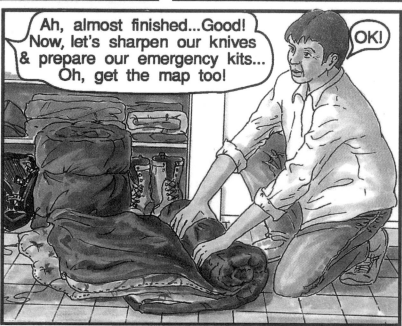

Ah, almost finished...Good! Now, let's sharpen our knives & prepare our emergency kits... Oh, get the map too!

OK!

Chris makes up his Emergency Kit, everything but the matches.

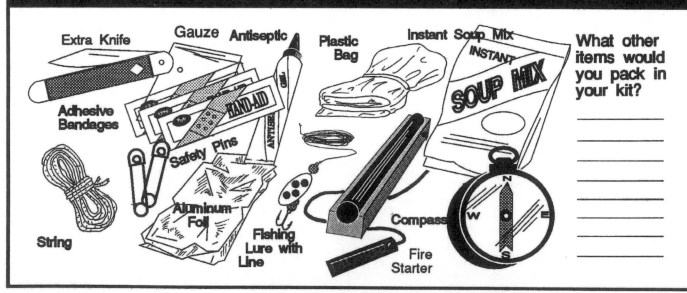

Extra Knife
Gauze
Antiseptic
Plastic Bag
Instant Soup Mix
INSTANT
SOUP MIX

Adhesive Bandages
HAND-AID
Safety Pins
Aluminum Foil
Fishing Lure with Line
String
Fire Starter
Compass

What other items would you pack in your kit?

_____
_____
_____
_____
_____
_____
_____

Chris, here's this years hunting regulations, I want you to take time and read it.

HUNTING REGULATIONS

Will Do!

Why does Chris' dad want him to read the Hunting Regulations?

☐ He wants Chris to become familiar with the Hunting Regulations?

☐ He wants Chris to understand fully the Hunting Regulations of their state? ❸

Chris' dad marks a map to leave at home showing where they will be camped and the general area they will be hunting. Why is this a good idea?

We'll be hunting in this general area and camped here by Crystal Creek.

As the final items are packed carefully and securely in the truck...

Here's the last one Dad... are we about ready to go?

We Sure Are! Now to swing over and pick up your Uncle Ted... and We're On Our Way!

There's Uncle Ted...Looks like he's all ready to go!

Hi Uncle Ted have you been waiting long?

Yeh, I've been waiting since deer season last year!

AT LAST, now with everything loaded, the rifles in their cases and packed safely behind the seat, they are finally... ON THEIR WAY!

Did they do the right thing by putting the guns in their cases inside the truck behind the seat?

Hey, I found out that Mr. Williams has put up a gate & NO TRESPASSING signs on the road we usually use. He may not let us go through!

I'll bet he will let us... Let's ask him!

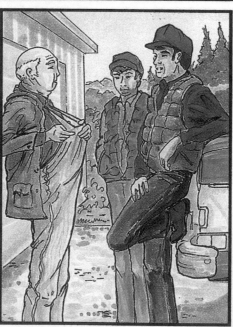

Well...being you asked me friendly like, go ahead. Just close the gates behind ya!

What if...

the Landowner had refused to let them use the road?
What do you think they should do?

☐ Go through anyway.

☐ Wait until dark and then go through.

☐ Find an alternate area to hunt in. ❹

Camps about set up & Chris has arranged the rocks around the designated fire area. His dad has been chopping firewood and Uncle Ted is finishing unloading the truck. Supper is next, and then relax around the campfire & tell wild and wonderful hunting stories.

As the campfire flickers brightly, the stories have filled Chris' head with great anticipation and excitment of tomorrows hunt...

O-O-O-AH!

I think I'll hit the sack!

NEW WORLD RECORD

"CHRIS... Time to get UP!"

As Chris sticks his head out into the brisk morning air... the smell of something wonderful!

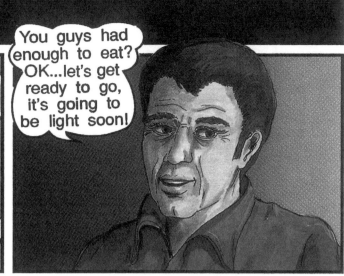

BACON... EGGS... HASH BROWNS

You guys had enough to eat? OK...let's get ready to go, it's going to be light soon!

Last Minute Check...

- ☐ Plenty of Ammunition
- ☐ Knife, Rope, Emergency Kit, Lunch Items, Hunting License.
- ☐ Canteen with fresh water.
- ☐ First aid items
- ☐ Everything put away in the camp, tent secured.
- ☐ Breakfast fire completely put out!
- ☐ Adequate clothing for todays weather.

Can you think of anything else you should check on before you leave camp?

WHY
is it important to find an obvious landmark and to always know where it is?

Chris' Dad tells him to observe where they are going in regards to that mountain. He tells him that their camp is located just down and in front of the cliffs of the mountain, which is East.

What other landmarks could you use?

_____

_____

_____

Chris, I'll go on this side of the canyon, Ted will be on the other side and you stay in the middle. We'll work slowly down...Don't be in a hurry...go slow and keep your eyes and ears open. Give us a few minutes head start and then you start down. Try to stay about even as we go. We should be back in camp about mid afternoon. OK?

Chris waits...

Then Chris starts down slowly... When he hears something! HE STOPS...WHAT IS IT?

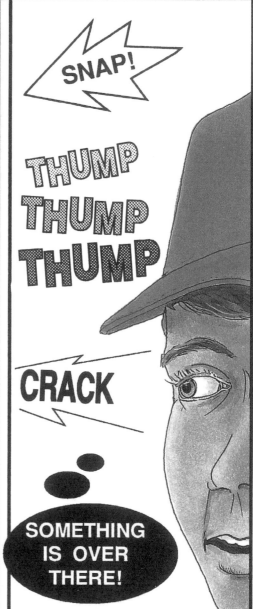

SNAP!

THUMP
THUMP
THUMP

CRACK

SOMETHING IS OVER THERE!

There is definitely something moving in the thick brush...Maybe its a DEER! What should he do?

- [ ] Fire at the movement in the brush?
- [ ] Shoot into the trees to scare it out into the open?
- [ ] Make sure as to what it is before he even raises his rifle?

5

Snap!

IT'S HIS DAD!!!

Now, Chris sees why you should be **ABSOLUTELY SURE** of your target. NEVER...NEVER... shoot at anything **UNLESS YOU ARE**

100% SURE

Chris continues on...

When the unexpected HAPPENS!!!

He has taken a pretty good fall, but he is OK...A little scratch on his hand but with a bandaid and disinfectant from his emergency kit everything is fine. There are 2 things he must do right now before going on any further. WHAT ARE THEY? 1._____ 2._____

1. MAKE SURE THAT THERE IS NOTHING IN THE BARREL OF THE RIFLE.

2. TAKE TIME TO MAKE SURE EVERYTHING IS IN GOOD WORKING ORDER, AND NO DIRT AROUND THE BOLT OR ON THE SCOPE.

He walks down a little further to the edge of some pines, leans back against a log... when he hears something again... This time its behind him! He Looks Back...

A DEER! Ahhh... Its a doe...But hold it there's another one there in the trees... Maybe...Maybe... I Hope...I Hope... Be still... Just be calm.. Easy does it now...

Ever so cautious,
out he steps...
A Big
Beautiful **BUCK!!!**

He Sees Chris!
He Freezes in
His Tracks...
Chris slowly
raises his rifle...

Slides the
safety off...

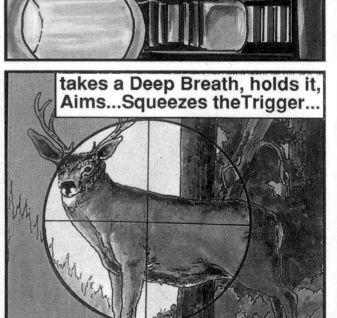

takes a Deep Breath, holds it,
Aims...Squeezes theTrigger...

KER-POW

HE'S HIT! HE'S HIT! Chris Quickly Bolts Another Shell into the Chamber!

CLAK CLAK

The Buck Suddenly Lunges, Spins and CRASHES OFF into the Heavy, Thick Timber!

Meanwhile...

Chris' Dad and Ted have bagged a nice forked horn and are dressing it when...

There's a shot! Probably at that big buck we jumped further back...You don't suppose Chris?...Na-a-aw!

Could be, I think he's still back of us!

Chris places his rifle on safety and scrambles up the hill to where the deer was standing when it was hit. He starts out in the direction that he last saw the buck heading. He looks for tracks and also any signs of blood.

Chris continues on, when there in the trail, on a log he sees...

BLOOD!

Keeping his eyes on the deer tracks, he anxiously hurries on, with not one thought as to the time and the distance he has gone. nor in the direction that he is headed.

In his excitement Chris has over-looked an important rule. What is it? ⑥

☐ To always know which direction camp is located.

☐ Losing track of the original landmark.

☐ He failed to set new landmarks for himself so he could back track to where he started when he shot the deer.

Chris approaches the deer cautiously, picks up a long stick and touches the deer in the area above the eye. The eye of the deer doesn't blink which tells him that the deer is dead.
Is this a good thing to do? Yes■ No■

What is the very next thing Chris should do?

- ☐ He should take off as fast as he can and try to find his dad.

- ☐ He should immediately tag his deer.

- ☐ He should head out for camp and wait there for his dad.

- ☐ He should sit down and wait for his dad and Uncle Ted to come and help him.

- ☐ He should field dress the deer as quickly as possible.

- ☐ He should start dragging it back towards camp and clean it there.

7

Chris hangs his rifle and coat on a stout limb, out of the way, pushes up his sleaves and gets prepared for another first hand experience.

I think I'd better move him around clear of that rock so it will be easier to get at.

MAN! is he ever HEAVY!

BASIC FIELD DRESSING FUNDAMENTALS

1. Place deer on its back, and cut the penis sheath and testicle sack free and lay to one side. *(In some states or provinces you must leave these attached to carcass for proof of sex.)*

2. Carefully cut up the middle to the breast bone (be very careful not to puncture the stomach or any of the intestines).

3. Cut around the vent and tie with a piece of string, this will prevent any waste from getting into the cavity.

4. Now, with the intestines exposed, carefully remove the deer's bladder, be very careful not to puncture it, as this will taint the meat.

5. Next, cut the diaphragm (this is the thin muscle lining bewteen the body cavity and the chest cavity).

6. Cut free the organs from inside the chest cavity (heart and lungs).

7. Cut the esophagus and trachea as high up in the neck as possible.

8. Now, with a good grasp, pull until the esophagus and trachea are free and remove the organs and the entrails from the carcass.

Remember

PROPER CLEANING & CARE MEANS "GOOD EATING".

In some states it is illegal to leave entrals in the field. Be sure you know your states law.

Chris is lucky his deer is by some water, with the chest shot the deer has bled internally and the inside of the deer is very bloody. He uses his canteen cup and flushes out the inside of the deer until it is free of all the blood. The cold water from the stream will also help to cool down the carcass and help release the body heat.

Chris cuts out the liver, washes it off good and puts it in a plastic bag. "Liver'n Onions Tonight".

He carefully washes, dries his knife and puts it back in its sheath. <u>NEVER</u> lay your knife down, you just may lose it.

Chris raises the deer as high as he can and ties it securely. The deer's hind quarters are still laying on the ground, but Chris props it up as good as he can with a couple of short logs.

Next he props it open with a limb.

With a cloth, he wipes dry the inside.
Why do this?

He washes and dries his arms and hands.

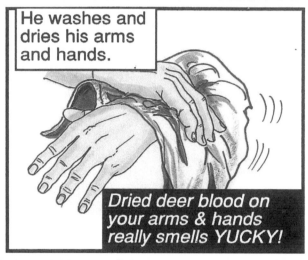

Dried deer blood on your arms & hands really smells YUCKY!

ALL DONE! Now I'll go and find Dad and Ted. Man, will they be SURPRISED!

As Chris heads back, he stops by the big rock for a second...he looks up & notices something that he wasn't aware of before. Why should he be concerned?

He hikes along but stops <u>short of the ridge</u> and takes a breather.

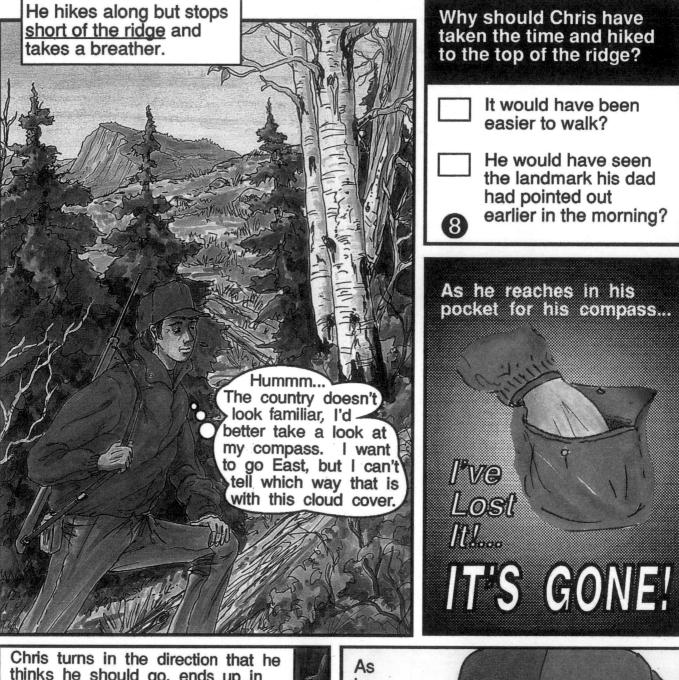

Hummm... The country doesn't look familiar, I'd better take a look at my compass. I want to go East, but I can't tell which way that is with this cloud cover.

Why should Chris have taken the time and hiked to the top of the ridge?

☐ It would have been easier to walk?

☐ He would have seen the landmark his dad had pointed out earlier in the morning?

8

As he reaches in his pocket for his compass...

I've Lost It!....

IT'S GONE!

Chris turns in the direction that he thinks he should go, ends up in some real heavy, thick, timber...

AAH! There's a clearing ahead!!

As he steps into the open...

Oh-Oh!

Meanwhile...
Chris' Dad and Ted have made it back to camp with their deer, and when Chris is not there, there is some concern. His dad turns to Ted and says...

Ted, I'm a little worried about Chris, I think we'd better go out and look for him.

Good Idea! The clouds are getting darker too!

They start out...When in the distance...

POW POW POW

THEY STOP

They heard the 3 shots Chris just fired! Then they walk into the open...

Do you suppose that was Chris Signaling?

Could be... I'll answer back with two shots!

WHAM!

WHAM!

=POW — POW

Chris eagerly gathers some firewood for his fire and doesn't hear the answer back to his signal.

This will be enough to get a good one started!

CRA-A-ACK SNAP!

If Chris had heard the two answer shots he should have then...

☐ Fired three more shots in return into a Stump?

☐ Started out in the general direction he <u>thought</u> the shots came from?

☐ Not waste any more shells?

 9

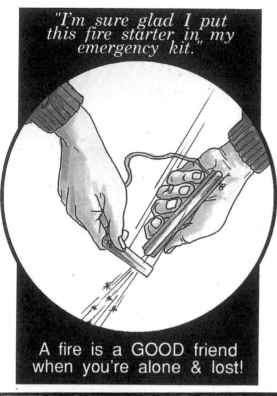

"I'm sure glad I put this fire starter in my emergency kit."

A fire is a GOOD friend when you're alone & lost!

I'm getting hungry...Hey, I've got some soup mix in my pack...Ah, Hot Soup

Smells good already, but I could sure go for a T-bone Steak!

Hey, that was a FISH THAT JUMPED...There's a fishing lure in my kit... I'll bet I could catch him!

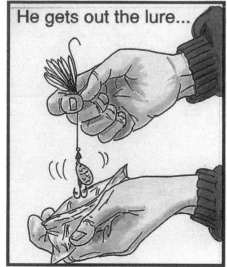

He gets out the lure...

cuts a green limb...

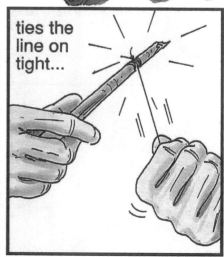

ties the line on tight...

Good Grief thats **SNOW!**

i'D BETTER BUILD ME A SHELTER & QUICK!

Chris quickly gathers a bunch of pine bows...

I know I shouldn't break limbs off trees... but this is an emergency! Maybe even a matter of LIFE OR DEATH!!

he rounds up some logs to make a frame...

connects them together...

tops if off with the pine bows...

IT MIGHT SNOW 3 FEET DEEP!

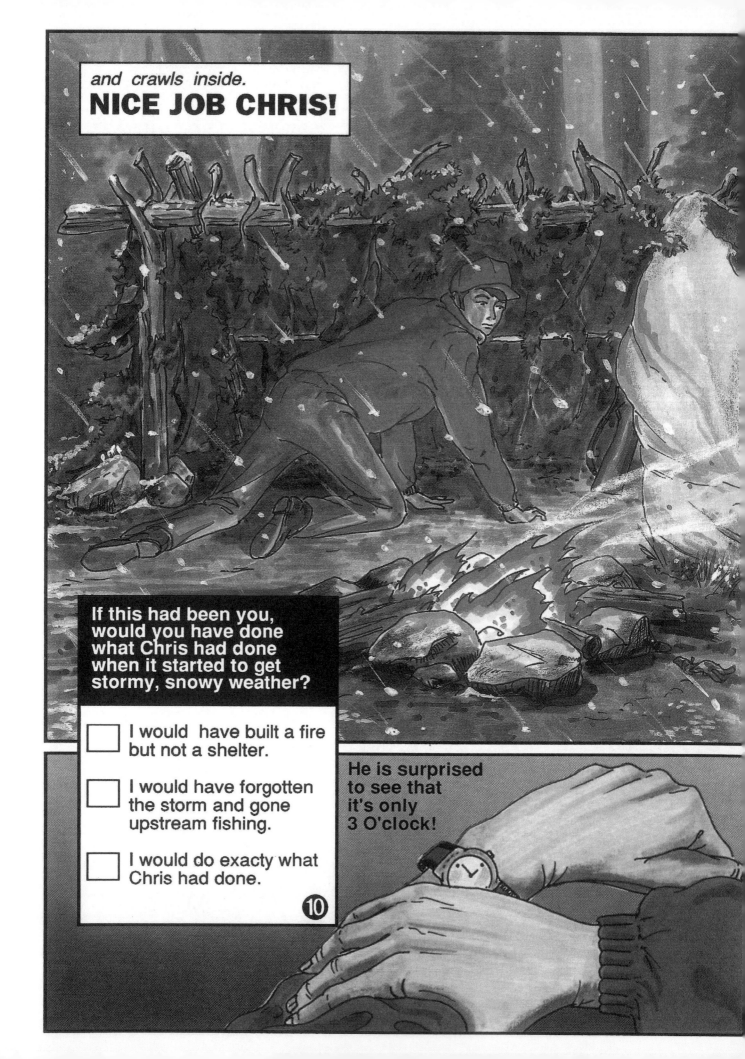

Meanwhile...

Higher up on the mountain the winds are stronger, snow is heavier. Chris' dad and Ted have found shelter in some dense pines just down from the top of the ridge.

Hey, Ted... over there is a patch of blue sky...looks like this storm is blowing over. Let's get up on the ridge and take a Look-See!

Ted, there's a campfire down there!

Let's check it out!

BACK TO CHRIS

He hears some Weird Noises...

CRACK! THUD

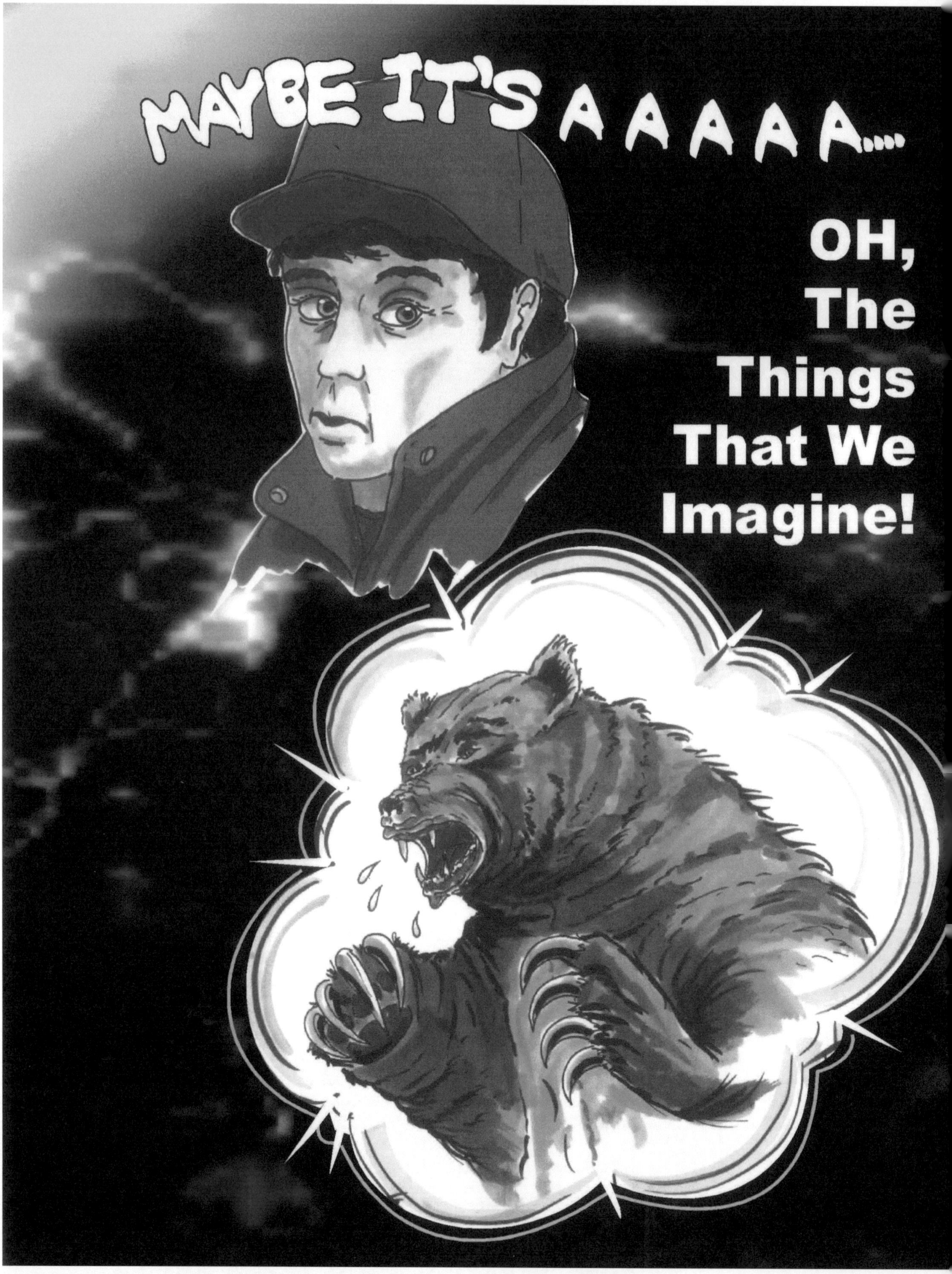
MAYBE IT'S A A A A A....
OH, The Things That We Imagine!

As the dark clouds break away & the late afernoon sun breaks through...OUT THE CREATURE STEPS!

Oh...WOW! Some Ferocious Monster You Are!

YO, DAD OVER HERE!

Hey, Chris are you OK?

Sure!

Dad...Sorry I got lost... but I...

Hey...No problem, anyone can get lost... You did what was smart...You stayed in one place. YOU DID THE RIGHT THING... AND I'M PROUD OF YOU!!

Take a look at this shelter he built!

My First Hunting Adventure

Name_____

My First Hunting Year was_____

I went hunting with_____

The Place I went hunting was_____

I Shot_____Times.

I Bagged a_____

The Most Exciting Time
Was when I_____
_____
_____
_____

My First Hunt was
Enjoyable because

_____
_____
_____

Things I will always remember about my first hunt

_____
_____
_____

TO THE PARENTS:
Save this book along with your
hunters comments and their
photo for memorable recollections
in the years to come.

Place
Photo
Here

ANSWERS TO THE MULTIPLE CHOICE QUESTIONS

❶ He wanted him to become familiar
With his new rifle.
❷ All answers are correct.
❸ Both answers are correct.
❹ Find an alternate area to hunt.
❺ Make sure as to what it is before he even
raises his rifle.
❻ All answers are correct.

❼ He should immediately tag his deer.
He should field dress the deer as quickly as
possible.
❽ He would have seen the landmark his
Dad had pointed out to him.
❾ **Fired three shots in return into a Stump.**
❿ I would do exactly what Chris had done.

Printed in the United States
by Baker & Taylor Publisher Services